Fight the Invaders!

PATHFINDER EDITION

By Lana Costantini and Kirsten Weir

CONTENTS

THE INVADERS

Armies of creatures are on the move in places where they don't belong. They kill the animals and plants that get in their way. Is there any way to stop them?

By Lana Costantini

Giant cane toad

Imagine this: A crocodile and a toad the size of a dinner plate come face-to-face on a riverbank. The croc attacks the toad. Who will win? You might be surprised. Yes, the croc eats the toad; yet within hours, the unlucky croc is dead, too. It met a deadly invader: the giant cane toad.

Cane toads are a huge problem in Australia—and not just for the crocs. People first brought the toads there in 1935, hoping the toads would prey on a sugarcane-eating beetle. Instead, the toads ate everything in sight. They feasted on insects, frogs, and even birds' eggs. They ate so much that there wasn't much left for native animals to eat.

And if that weren't enough, people discovered that the cane toad also has a secret weapon; warts on its skin ooze a milky white poison. The cane toad's toxic body kills larger animals that eat it, like the croc.

With few enemies to stop them, cane toads have invaded much of northeastern Australia, and scientists are worried. Unless the toads are stopped, many of Australia's native animals may disappear forever.

Aliens Among Us

An **alien** invasion is taking place on Earth. The aliens aren't creatures from outer space; they are animals and plants from our own planet! They hop, slither, swim, and are carried to places they don't belong.

In their original homes, or ecosystems, these animals fit right in. Ecosystems often have a natural balance of predator and prey. However, if a new animal moves in, this balance can be seriously upset.

Sometimes invaders travel thousands of miles to get to their new homes. How do they manage to go so far? Often, people move plants and animals on purpose, like the cane toad. That was a mistake! Other creatures hitch rides on ships and airplanes. Some people set pets free when the animals get too big or too dangerous to handle.

All **invasive** animals are alike in one way, however. They thrive in their new homes.

Munch Break. *Up to 30 million nutria live in Louisiana's wetlands.*

Potent Rodent

Imagine a swimming rodent the size of a small dog. Meet the nutria. It is destroying wetlands in the United States, especially in the Southeast.

People first brought nutria to the U.S. from South America in the 1930s. Farmers bred them for their fur. Some nutria escaped into wild marshes. Without South America's severe weather to battle, they thrived.

Now, millions of nutria munch on marsh grasses across the U.S. They rip out the plants by the roots, causing the soil to wash away. No soil means that new plants can't grow. Baby fish and crabs have fewer places to hide, and birds have fewer places to nest. Without the plants, it's much harder for them to survive. Many of these creatures now are endangered, or close to becoming extinct.

Lion of the Sea

Along the Atlantic Ocean's coral reefs, red lionfish are on the hunt. These newcomers have long, graceful fins that they use to herd fish into a small place. Then they gobble up the fish.

That's a big problem. Lionfish live naturally in the South Pacific Ocean, where many smaller fish have learned how to avoid them. Some large fish in the Pacific even eat lionfish.

In the Atlantic, however, lionfish have no natural enemies. They can kill as many as 80 percent of the native fish in a coral reef there. Human divers also better watch out. The lionfish's needle-shaped fins are full of poison. Ouch!

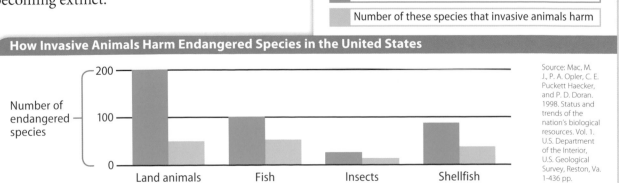

Total number of endangered species

Number of these species that invasive animals harm

How Invasive Animals Harm Endangered Species in the United States

Number of endangered species

200

100

0

Land animals | Fish | Insects | Shellfish

Source: Mac, M. J., P. A. Opler, C. E. Puckett Haecker, and P. D. Doran. 1998. Status and trends of the nation's biological resources. Vol. 1. U.S. Department of the Interior, U.S. Geological Survey, Reston, Va. 1-436 pp.

Loosed Lions. *Scientists think some pet owners set their lionfish loose in the Atlantic.*

Killer Beetles

In Michigan and nearby states, bug traps hang in backyards and forests. They capture a small but deadly **pest**—the emerald ash borer. This bright green beetle is native to Asia. First seen in Michigan in 2002, it may have traveled there in firewood.

The adult beetle chews on the leaves of ash trees and does little damage. It's the babies that are deadly. The worm-like larvae hatch under the bark of ash trees and eat the bark's inner layer. Without the inner bark, the trees can't get enough water and food. So far, the emerald ash borer has destroyed more than 30 million ash trees in Michigan alone!

Scientists Fight Back

Once invasive species move in, it's very hard to get rid of them. People in Australia have spent more than $15 million fighting cane toads. Now, scientists may have a new weapon. They discovered the toads die after eating Australia's lavender beetles. They hope to find a way to use the beetle to fight the toad.

People set traps to catch some nutria and emerald ash borers. Lionfish pose a bigger challenge. No one knows exactly how to keep them from spreading in the open ocean.

Scientists won't—indeed, they can't—give up. Too many species have become extinct or are at risk of dying out, thanks to these invaders. If they aren't stopped, what will happen?

Tree Pest. *The emerald ash borer came from Asia and has spread to ten U.S. states and parts of Canada.*

WORDWISE

alien: belonging to a different place, foreign

invasive: tending to spread actively or aggressively

pest: an animal that causes problems for people

TINY INVADERS

BY KIRSTEN WEIR

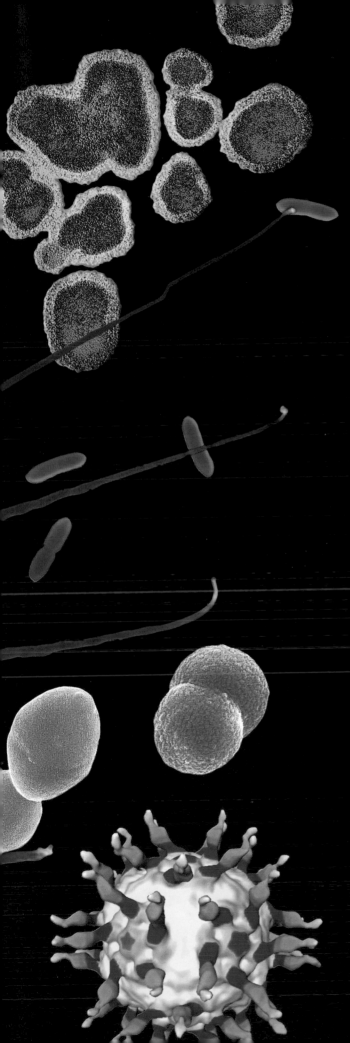

Have you ever been sick?

Perhaps you felt cruddy from a cold, or maybe your stomach ached for hours. It wasn't fun, was it?

Getting sick is a pain. Sure, you get to stay home from school. That can be nice— for a while. Still, troubled tummies, scratchy throats, and runny noses usually mean one thing: germs!

Germs are tiny invaders. They get into your body and make you sick. Luckily, your body works hard to keep you from getting sick. Read on to find out how.

A World of Germs

The germs that make you sick are lurking everywhere. They are sitting on your desk, hiding on this page, even floating in the air that you are breathing.

What's worse, these germs and the sicknesses they cause are getting around faster than ever. How? People travel more these days. They fly to faraway mountains and trek to distant jungles, taking their germs with them.

People aren't the only things moving around. Plants and animals move around, too. Some germs go along for the ride.

There's another reason that diseases are spreading; Earth is heating up. Animals such as mosquitoes like the heat, so they are moving into areas that are getting warmer. These pests often carry germs that can make you sick.

Under Your Skin

How can you protect yourself from dangerous germs? You may not know it, but you have a germ-fighting weapon: your own body!

Your body's first line of defense is your skin. It acts like armor, blocking some **viruses**. Viruses can cause the flu and chickenpox, as well as more serious diseases such as smallpox and hepatitis.

Your skin also blocks tiny creatures called bacteria. Bacteria can cause sore throats, ear infections, and more serious diseases such as cholera and plague.

Sometimes germs do get past your skin. They can creep through cuts, sneak into scrapes, and ride on food. They can also enter your body when you touch your nose or mouth with dirty hands.

Fighting Back

You and your body can fight off these tiny invaders. Start by washing your hands with soap and water. Soap kills many germs, and water washes them away.

Washing your hands isn't always enough. Tricky germs can still find ways of attacking you. Luckily, you have an **immune system**— your body's second line of defense. Your immune system hunts down and destroys germs. How?

Special cells called white blood cells patrol your body. Some have big appetites for germs! Others make **antibodies**, which stick to germs.

There is a different antibody for each kind of germ. Some antibodies keep germs from making you sick, while others help your body find and kill germs.

After a germ is destroyed, the antibodies hang out in your body for a while. They protect you if the same kind of germ comes back. That way, you usually will not get the same illness twice.

Getting Your Shots

The immune system is pretty good at fighting germs, but sometimes it needs help. Luckily there are medicines called vaccines that can make your immune system stronger.

A vaccine contains germs that have been killed or weakened. The dead or dying germs can't make you sick. Instead, they trigger your body to make antibodies. If the same germ ever shows up again, then your antibodies attack it.

Kids usually get sick more often than adults. That's because kids haven't been **exposed** to as many germs, so they have fewer antibodies. Your body learns quickly, however. It's probably making antibodies right now.

Diseases may be spreading more easily these days, but don't worry too much. Your skin and immune system are always working to protect you.

From the Floor to Your Sandwich

If you drop a piece of bread on the floor but pick it up within five seconds, is it still safe to eat? No! Bacteria are transferred immediately, no matter how quickly you react. How many bacteria stick? That depends on how long the bacteria have been on the floor.

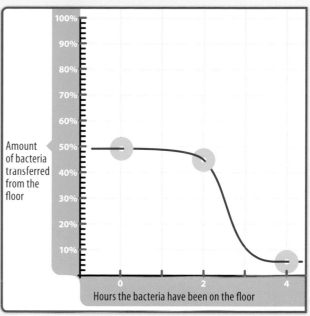

Source: Dawson, P., I. Han, M. Cox, C. Black, and L. Simmons, "Residence time and food contact time effects on transfer of *Salmonella* Typhimurium from tile, wood and carpet: testing the five-second rule," *Journal of Applied Microbiology* 102 (2007): 945.

On the Hunt.
The large pink cell is hunting the green bacteria.

Wordwise

antibody: substance that attacks invaders in your body

exposed: made open to something

immune system: parts of your body that fight disease

virus: germ that can live only inside an animal or plant

FIGHTING BACK

Your skin and your cells help protect you from germs. This diagram shows how.

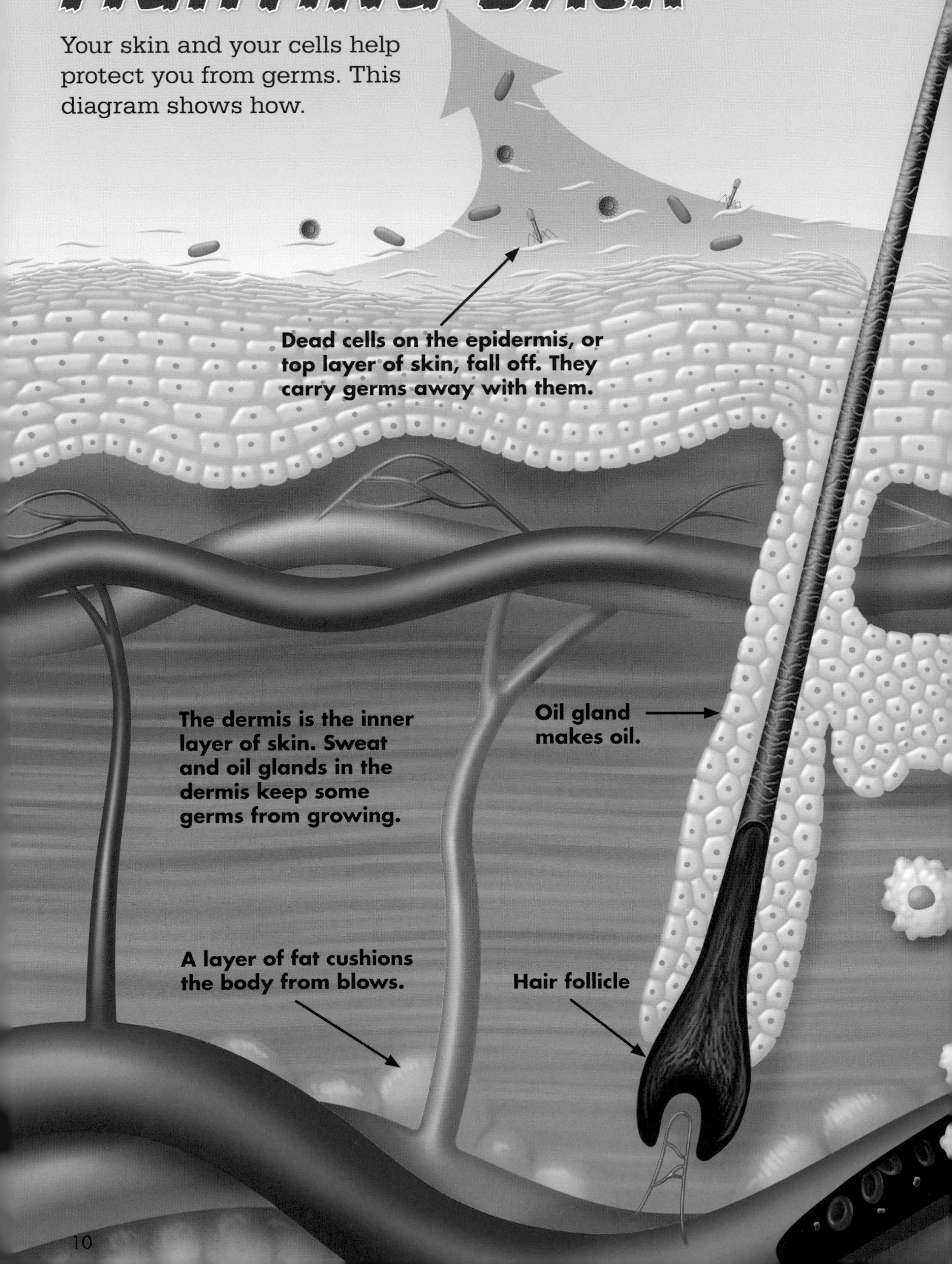

Dead cells on the epidermis, or top layer of skin, fall off. They carry germs away with them.

The dermis is the inner layer of skin. Sweat and oil glands in the dermis keep some germs from growing.

Oil gland makes oil.

A layer of fat cushions the body from blows.

Hair follicle

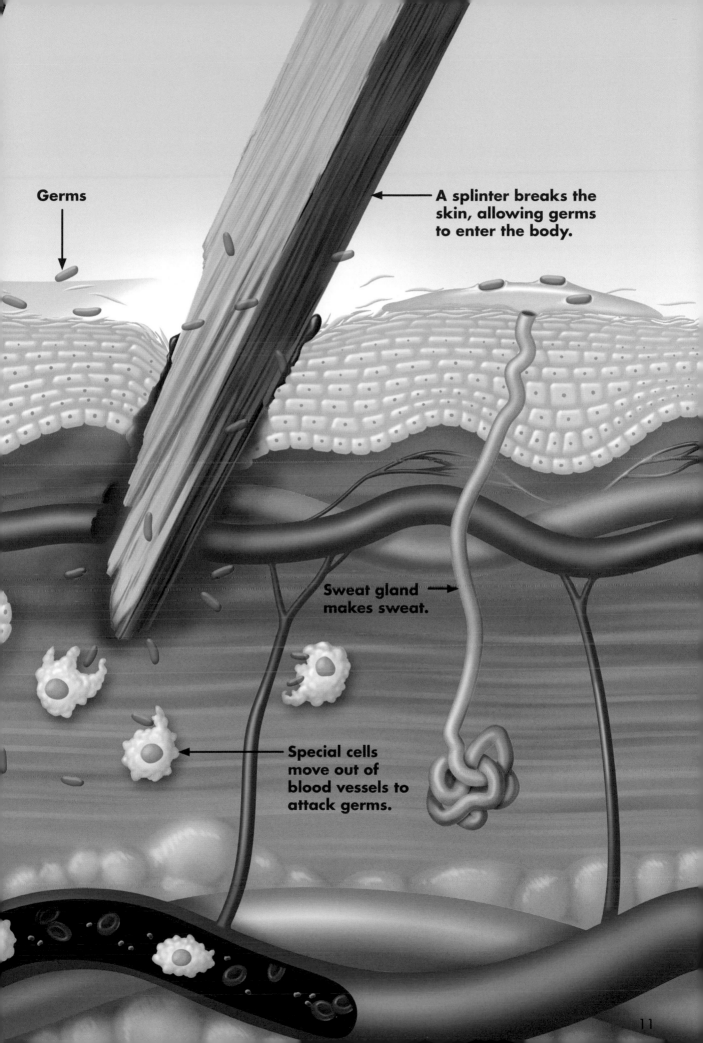

Germs

A splinter breaks the skin, allowing germs to enter the body.

Sweat gland makes sweat.

Special cells move out of blood vessels to attack germs.

11

Invasion!

It's time to fight back. Answer these questions to show what you know about invaders.

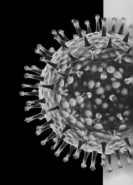

1 Why are invasive species a problem? How can the problem be solved?

2 Study the graph on page 4. What living things do invaders harm most?

3 Why do germs spread around the world more quickly today?

4 How does your body fight germs? How do you fight germs with your choices?

5 What do lavender beetles and antibodies have in common?

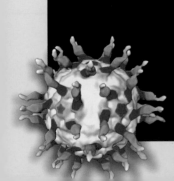